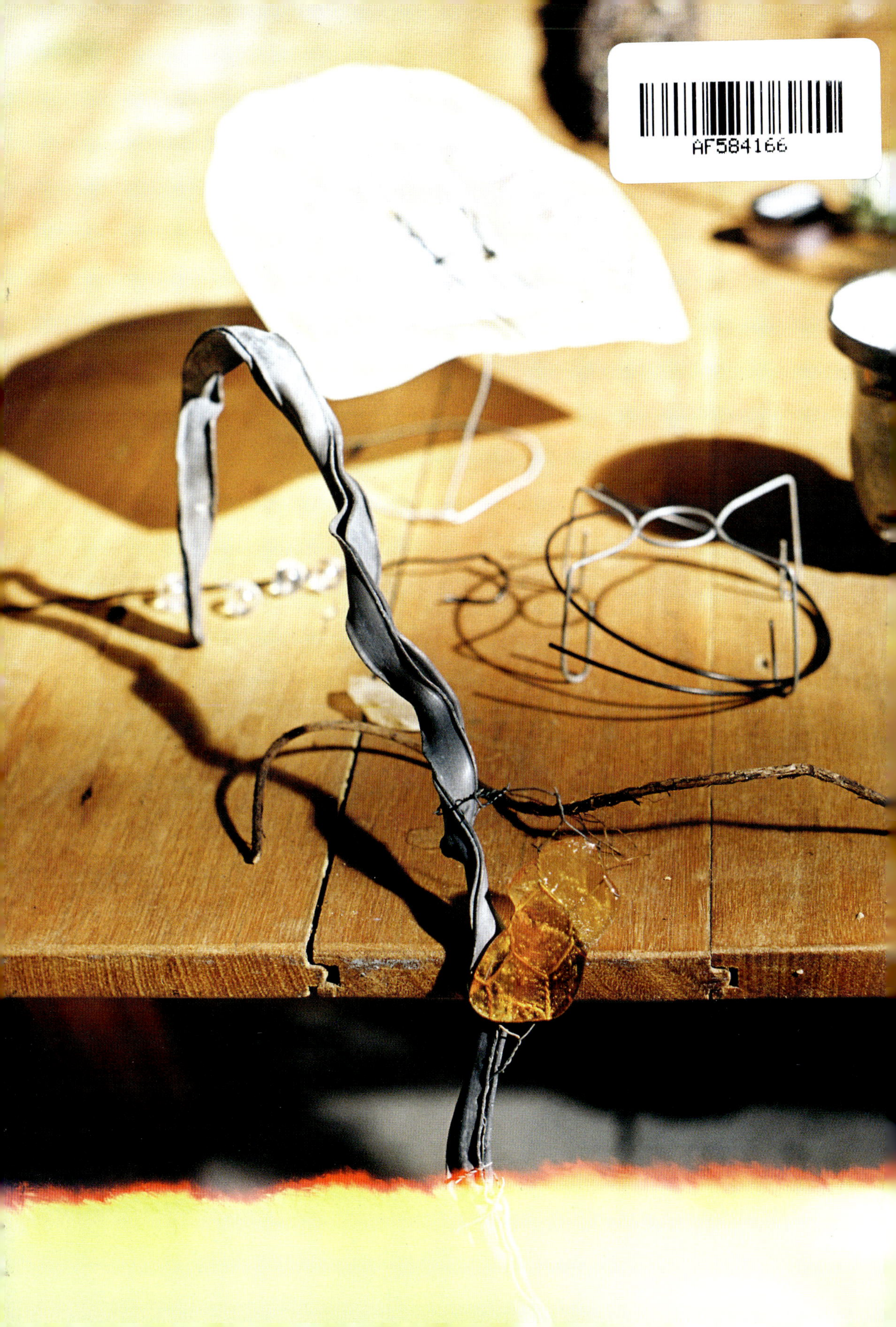

Brighid Fitzgerald and Amy Jane Parker work in close proximity with one another. They share a studio (along with painter Clare Longley) in Coburg, as well a range of artistic interests. These include ecological thinking, the afterlives of waste, and the transmutation of materials over time. Often unfurling in parallel, sometimes their practices converge. In 2019 they co-curated *Whorled* as part of the Hobienniale in nipulina/Hobart, for which they transformed the former Forestry Tasmania building into an immersive exhibition complete with a gravel pathway that circled around the building's central structural column. The building used to house a plantation of native trees—a propaganda exercise intended to offset criticism of the company's ecocidal felling of old-growth forests. (This interior forest has since been deforested too.) The following year, in 2020, Fitzgerald and Parker planned a self-directed residency at the site of Agnes Denes's *Forest for Australia* (1998), a land artwork comprising 6000 native trees planted in five concentric circular shapes at City West Water's Altona Treatment Plant. (Denes's work is another kind of failed forest, as its plantation coincided with a decade-long drought and several of the species planted were specific to the continent but not the Country, and thus struggled with soil salinity levels.) And more recently, in 2021, the artists collaborated on a series of bookmarks, which they titled *Pulsemarks*, as a satellite project for *Micro-(bial) Tenancies* curated by Abbra Kotlarczyk at Blindside Gallery.

For this exhibition at Mejia, Brighid and Amy present two distinct bodies of work side by side. Brighid's pivots around a very specific material: tree roots that grew through the sewerage pipes of her family home over the past three decades (that is, her lifespan). The roots were dislodged from the pipes by her father and, on request, dutifully rain washed, sun dried, and stored on an open-air chicken wire hammock. In the exhibition, these roots come into contact with a range of other materials through sculptural assemblage: tree guards for young saplings; green peridot collected from the gravel quarry used to make the road leading to/from her family home and to/from the sea; shimmering, midnight-blue eyeshadow and tear-drop diamantes; hula hoops; balls of petrol clumped together and spewed up by the ocean (a black sticky substance that Brighid collects, having initially mistaken it for ambergris washed up along shorelines); transparent glass beads; and strands of her own hair.

Interlocking Borromean knots appear in several of Brighid's sculptures. These reference the artist's commitment to psychoanalysis, which she undertakes in tandem or 'side by side' with her studio practice. What both practices have in common for her is the act of 'surfacing'—a ladder-like movement up 'from the depths.' For Lacan, the Borromean knot describes a nonhierarchical topology in which the real, the symbolic, and the imaginary of the subject are interlinked. For Brighid, it is a structure through which external elements enter her practice.

Where knots proliferate in Brighid's work, loops, twirls, and whirls course throughout Amy's. The body of work she presents at Mejia broadly concerns processes of queer gestation, marking a subtle turning point from earlier works that explored processes of digestion. In doing so, Amy's work continues to dissolve the boundary that demarcates the end of one body and the beginning of another—whether human or non-human. The twisted lead and glass work that trails down from Mejia's ceiling beam can be read as a deconstructed lead-light window, referencing medieval Christian theology in which the Virgin's womb was believed to be made of glass, crystal, pearl, amber, and other hard gems—a proto-cyborg of sorts. These materials have been embedded in the folds of lead, referencing non-human forms of gestation, like the way a pearl will form around an irritant such as a grain of sand.

The twisting, looping form of the lead, which is further echoed in a ceramic work displayed on the floor where it couches small pools of oil (*elselslelslelselselse,* 2022), has recurred regularly in her work since first appearing as the title of her 2017 exhibition at Punk Cafe, *elselselselselselse (running else).* Like this sibilant concrete poem, Amy's sculptures winnow away the spaces and separations between discrete entities, instead favouring models of imbrication, interaction, and endlessness.

This publication has been produced over the course of the exhibition and functions, like the exhibition, simply to hold these two different bodies of work together. In keeping with the spirit of Amy and Brighid's practices, these bodies of work are here rendered capacious by the introduction of several more voices and artworks into their fold.

First and foremost, Brighid and Amy's artworks are framed by and held within photographs taken by the artist Beth Maslen, who works across sculpture and photography herself, and who shot several rolls of film both in the studio and the gallery, capturing intimate spatial relationships, the encroachment of matter outside the work, and, most importantly, light as a connective tissue between all three artists' chosen media (glass, tree roots, photography).

Interviews conducted with Brighid and Amy include ruminations on their materials, processes, and enduring concerns, whilst conjuring more voices from their personal archives — from Hélène Cixous to Heather Davis.

A suite of poems by writer, editor, and artist Chi Tran index another shared history between Brighid and Amy, in that both share an abiding admiration of Chi's work and have commissioned poems by them for previous exhibitions. Chi's research interest in 'language as an active lifeform' resonates strongly in Brighid's approach to sculpture and speech as a form of ephemeral 'surfacing.' Chi's interest in genetic memory chimes with Amy's research into the transmutation of materials and the impossibility of matter ever disappearing; instead, it just changes form.

Writer and editor Autumn Royal has composed an ekphrastic poem in three parts for this publication, which describes an extended encounter with Brighid's sculpture *Bedside table*, itself a structure comprising the three interlinking rings of Lacan's Borromean knot. To write the poems, Autumn and Brighid spent hours sitting with the sculpture and talking through the ideas and processes behind and beside the work. But in reality, Autumn's writing reflects years of friendship and accumulated intimacy with, and insight into, the artist and her work. In this publication, Autumn's poems 'Approaching a bedside table I, II, and III' impress upon the reader key forms and functions of Brighid's work through sparse and subtle imagery: not only the knot, but the ladder, the lean, and the afterimage; the catching then inevitable letting-go of 'descriptions and narratives' that will but 'fall through' the flimsy structure that is the bedside table 'as it stands on points.'

From Paris, Aodhan Madden has contributed a new micro-fictional text in response to the themes and research underpinning Amy's work for Mejia — namely, concerning the Virgin Mary's womb as an architectonic and crystalline form. Aodhan's speculative fiction describes a stark theatrical stage setting that could be a cold, hard womb. The scene is populated by a chorus of slightly pathetic male figures — all of whom are struggling to come to terms with the uncertain contours of their subjectivity as en-wombed beings.

As Brighid reflected, the question of how (and whether) to bind this publication is also the question of the exhibition at Mejia. James Oates has brought considerable care and attention to the flow of texts and images, and overall formatting.

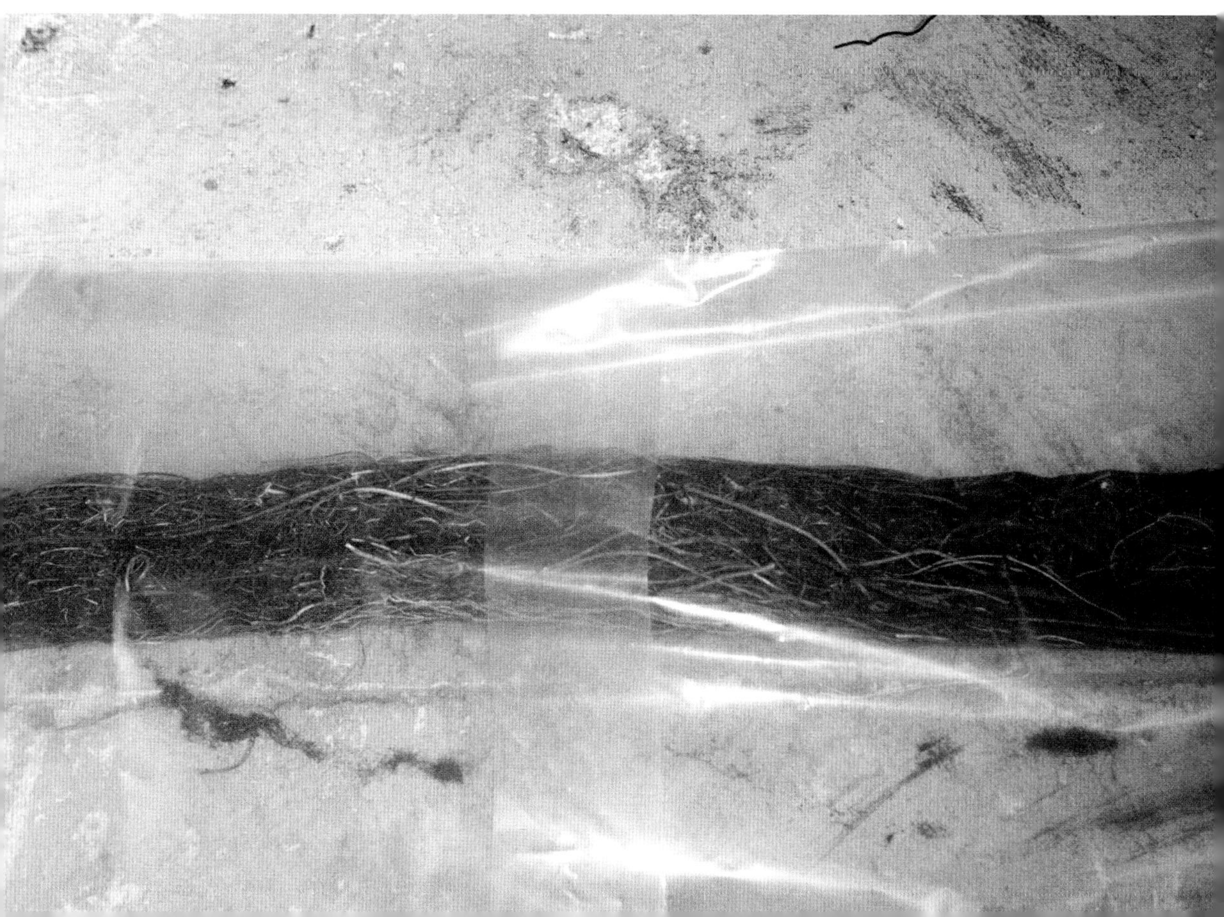

There is a desire to know your own history, to make mass
flatter and less obstructive.
I push myself to enact, emplace, configure — as a means
of finding some kind of 'lastingness.'
From where the neck curves into the shoulder, my body
enters a mode of speculation. And from this, I hope to
find a paradisiac way of building dimension, with the
freedom to move and where nothing ever happens.
There is a certain kind of catharsis that comes from the
collapse of a structure, perhaps within the learning that
we may continue to live without it.
So, while I have a tendency to mark all my intentions, I also
understand that to have the space to chew and uproot is
best — charging through movement, with the function of
allowing a course of change to take place out of sight.
I consider the idea of pouring water onto set concrete, as a
lesson in keeping the same person.
I sense a thing as a shape that matters, which is to say,
I suffuse it with utility, through my own experience.
Attention is a form of prayer, and there is no place like
home, like a body holding water.
There is a process through which we glean direction
spontaneously, in relation to another.
If we dissect a diagram of two or more people, we may begin
to see how a relationship becomes information.
It is difficult to refuse a distance between touching and
feeling, as we know the sky to be a hyper-object, and
identity too.

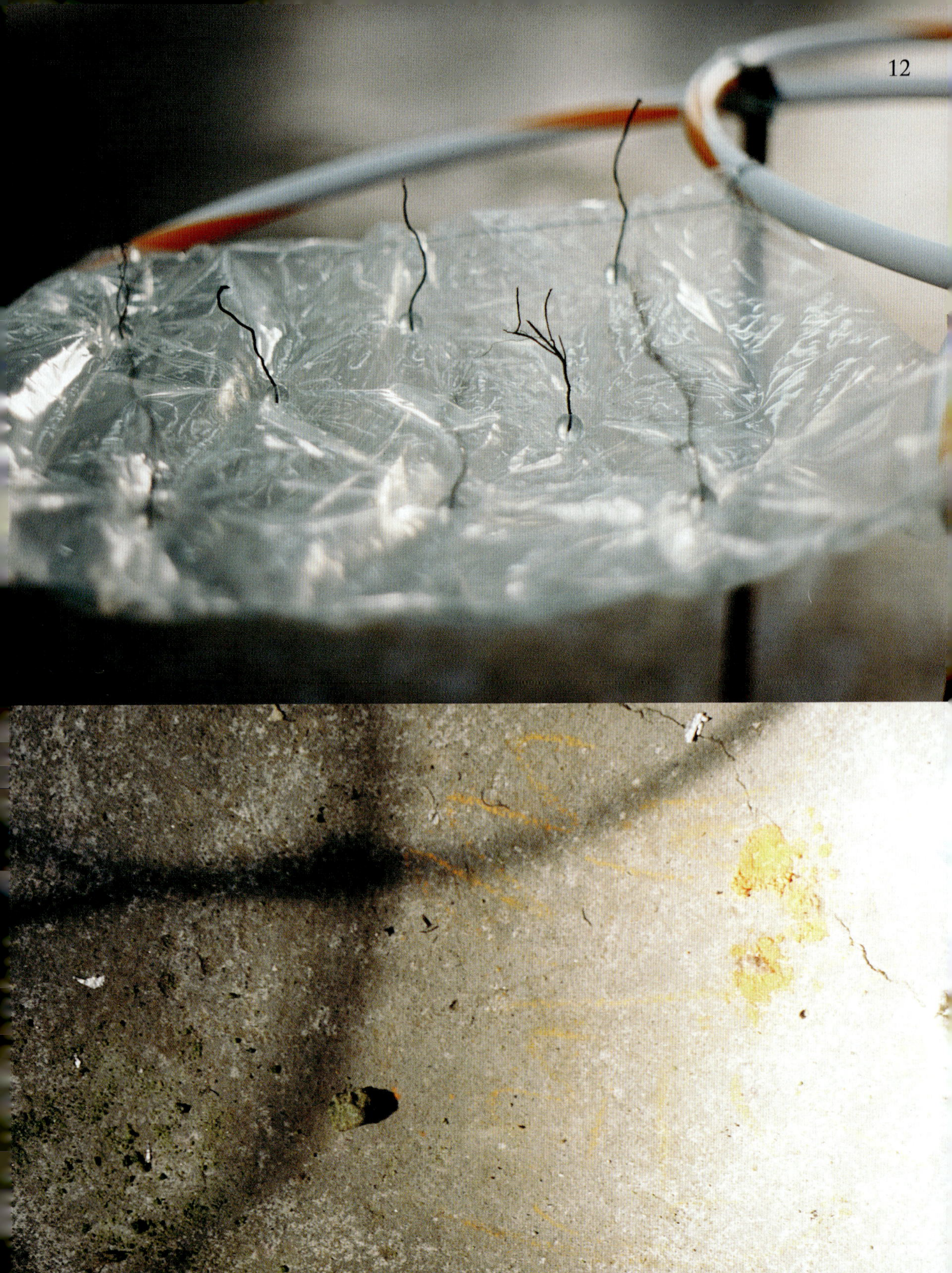

Approaching a bedside table I

Autumn Royal

'I dig my hands into the absolute. The surface
breaks' — Jorie Graham

You are assembled into a room,
the object of your gaze — a bedside table,
when you close your eyes, you sense
a violet mist beneath your lids —
it holds no obligations and is not
landscape — yet has come from many,
echo this as a way of letting go,
for reasons to mesh — flake against
this object — and that of a ladder
resting upright — but not definitively
against the bedside table.

Place a sheet over your regard,
obscuring any prior understandings
carried into the assembled room—
before applying glue, remember
how the last of daylight flashes green,
for an opening—rather than a waste,
in the sense of how the haircut makes
a haircut—the bedside table does not
ask permission as it stands on points—
all description and narrative
will fall through the bedside table.

Up against the wall — a bedside table
has been pushed and positioned —
the bedside table is not flat
yet it is against a wall, you turn away
a half-twist of attachment stops
you — knots into a turning back
toward the purpose of shifting
this position, it will loosen with time
as breath warms the surfaces
of hollows forming to hold all versions
assembled of the bedside table.

— after *Brighid Fitzgerald*

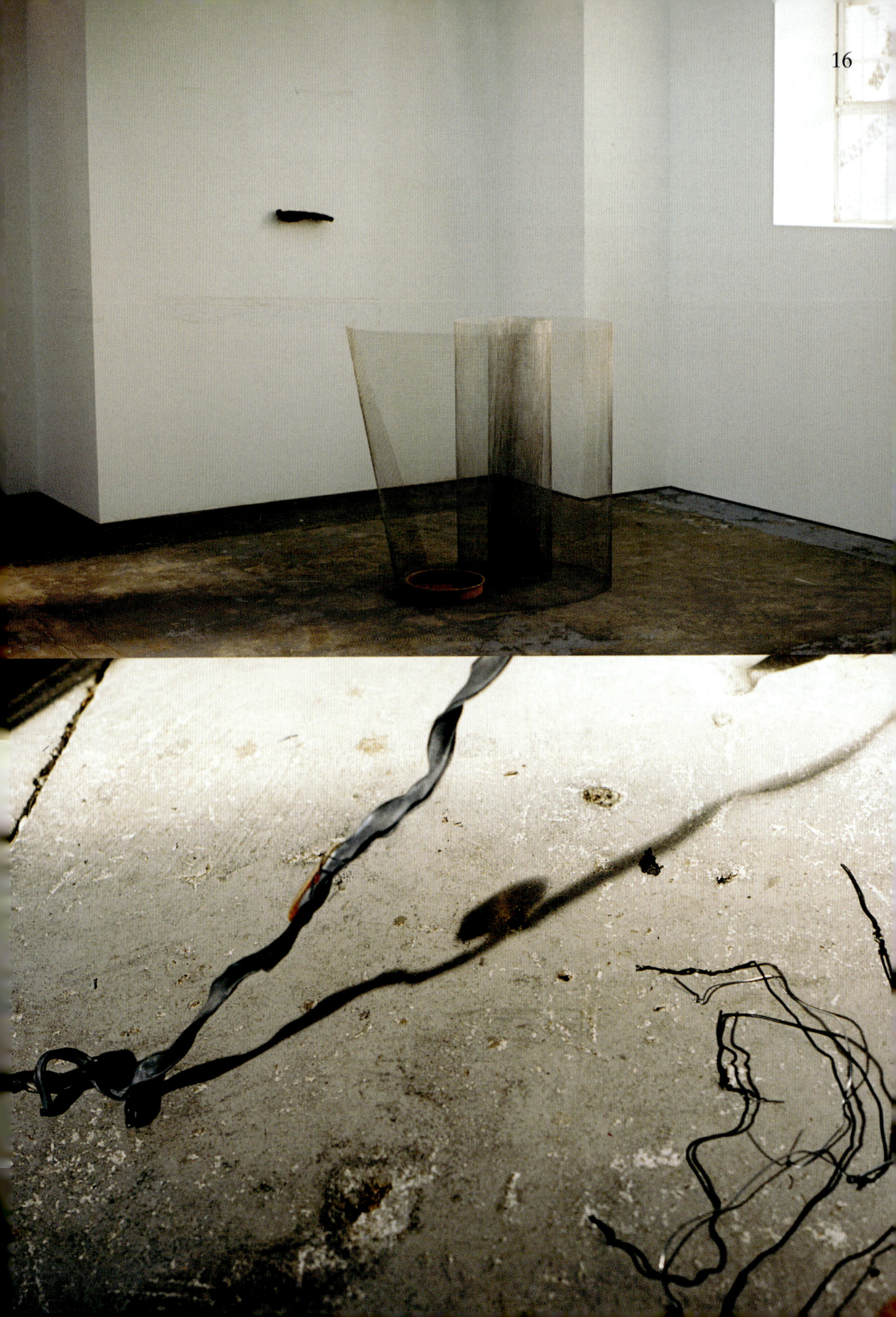

HH: In recent years, you have made ceramic sculptures that comprise tiny arms and hands. (Unfortunately, the one you made for this show didn't get fired in time!) I learned from you last week that these were made by pressing parts of the clay into a silicon cast of a statue of a pregnant woman, which you found outside a newsagency in Kensington. (The cast is just a fragment of the woman's hand touching her stomach.) What is interesting to me about these works—in relation to your work in this show—is the way you are thematising pregnancy outside the autobiographical format that we are so accustomed to encountering in canonical second- and even third-wave feminist artworks (Mary Kelly's *Post-partum document*, Amalia Ulman's Instagram project, I'm also thinking about the popularity of Maggie Nelson's *Argonauts* in the artworld more generally, etc.). Against autobiography, your work seems to open out into more deidentified, collectivised politics of gestation (thinking here of Sophie Lewis's *Full Surrogacy Now*, or Heather Davis, who you first introduced me to, and the idea that plastic waste is a kind of queer offspring that we have obligations to care for). Can you say more about how you're thinking about pregnancy and gestation in this body of work?

AJP: Yes, so the arms were first cast from a bizarre sculpture or monument of a heavily pregnant woman holding her stomach. There was a whole series of them in the window of this newsagency in Kensington, maybe twenty sculptures of varying configurations of very tall, very slender, nuclear families. There is also a man, seemingly her husband, holding this woman's stomach from behind, with a small child, pulling at her skirt or nestled between her legs. I was just intrigued by them as sculptures or trophies—that I couldn't really imagine ever being given or received—as intended at the instance of a new birth!

I think I continue to revisit Lewis's work because I've found her notion of family abolition something to reckon with. Lewis critiques the ways in which care and resources are systematically reserved and contained by the nuclear family in our heteronormative society. She advocates for a communism hinged on the abolition of the family, so that resources (material, social) can extend beyond these confines.

You're right, the work isn't autobiographical, and isn't considering gestation strictly in relation to humans either, but rather looks at reproduction and fertility/infertility across species. But these more abstract theories of Lewis's around the ownership or possession of children have definitely fed into personal conversations. As I'm in a relationship that will require a donation of sperm when/if we have children, we need to consider if the donor holds a sense of possession over the DNA and what that could mean. Or maybe we just welcome more dachshund crosses into our home! Lewis also explains that possessive individualism is linked to how resources are passed down via blood lines (inheritance), and as someone who will have an inheritance this has become personal and a means to think through how to manage that.

HH: I also have you to thank for introducing me to the *Electric Brine* reader, and the fantastic essay on amniotechnics by Sophie Lewis therein! Her idea about amniotechnics maybe marries some concerns explored in your earlier work—such as aquatic ecosystems, waste water, hydrofeminism, etc., etc.— with this new body of work. Between this past work and this new work, there seems to be a shift away from an exploration of processes of digestion and the way it changes matter almost alchemically (i.e., microplastics as broken down by Antarctic krill) to processes of gestation and reproduction.

AJP: Yes, definitely! And it was actually Chi who first introduced me (thanks

Chi). I love that phrase, electric brine — Lewis's description of the way in which all bodies are gestated underwater, in a mix of piss, water, shit, electrolytes, and fragments of DNA. I have been bathing ceramic forms in an electric brine of sorts over the past few years. Again, it's not autobiographical or thinking about gestation in the singular, but rather a means of thinking *through* these processes in an ecological sense, with material reference to our collective refuse, in the form of nanoplastics excreted from Antarctic krill.

I think the idea that underpins these theories, whether Lewis's amniotechnics or Astrida Neimanis's hydrofeminism, is a desire for 'maximum distribution of care based on the recognition that we all share substance.' This ultimately ecological view, focusing not only on the relation, but the imbrication of bodies stays with me, and although this current body of work is less wet, I hope it stays with the work too.

Yes, in the earlier work I was looking at digestion, not so much as metaphor I was quite literally working with digested matter. I began researching and working with the fecal matter of Antarctic krill back in 2019, when scientist and friend Sven Gauster introduced me to the research of his colleagues Rob King and So Kawaguchi at the Antarctic Division in nipulina. They were conducting a study of how krill were digesting oceanic microplastics, and with the aid of an extra set of teeth in the gullets and stomachs, macerating it into nano-form. It was first portrayed in the media as an epic enviro-win — the krill were finally solving/dissolving the waste of late capitalism. But of course, not quite the case, and the plastic's reduced size is rather more impactful. I'm always interested in how matter never really disappears; there's no such thing as 'elsewhere' in which it can be dispelled, rather it just changes form.

In the case of the nano-plastic, the plastic can now move through skin tissue, cells, and actually change DNA, materialising what Heather Davis describes as 'the becoming plastic of all biology.' I was really lucky to discuss this work with physicist Karan Barad when I was in nipulina, who said that when a material shifts scale in such a way, from the micro realm to the nano realm, the characteristics of the material are likely to totally shift as well. A material that is inert in atomic form may be reactive in nano form. The element gold, for example, isn't gold at all; it appears blood red at nanoscale.

It was the work of Davis that helped me to properly understand the ramifications of plastic on reproduction and fertility, and the queer potential of this. BPA is a plasticiser, systemic toxiciser, and endocrine disruptor that can affect the development of metabolic disorders such as low sex specific neurodevelopment. Davis points out how, in a sense, the absorption of plasticisers into bodies 'outpaces queer theory and sociopolitical movements that work to erode sexual difference.'

So, while this is more about potential infertility across species rather than gestation, while holding onto the severity and loss of extinction, Davis builds on the work of Haraway, describing the microbial beings evolving with the nano-plastic, through digestion, compelling us to consider these as 'non-filial progeny' of sorts. I'm interested in these beings — present in the assemblages but not visible — troubling these binaries of animate/inanimate, living or not. This idea of animacy, across materials, is a core interest of mine, and continues to propel the body of work that we are showing at Mejia.

HH: Some of our earliest conversations about this show pivoted around research you had been doing into medieval theories of the womb, which contrasts with the perceived abjection of repro-normative human wombs with the impossibly magical, gem-like womb of the Virgin Mary. What drew you to these ideas and what did they spark for you?

AJP: So, after spending a lot of time bathing works in literal shit (even though it sort of just looked like algae), I was really yearning to get out of the swamp! Anje

Piper, a friend who also spends a lot of time thinking about wombs, sent me medieval historian Lucy Allen Goss's research about a potentially queer, medieval depiction of Mary's womb. In this research, Goss positions Mary as 'proto-cyborg'—and her transparent, glass, self-medicalising womb as 'queering the womb.' This seemed like a gorgeous and glimmering way to continue exploring queer gestation!

I was first engrossed by the idea of this imagined womb as a sculpture; a complicated sculpture that, like Davis's and Lewis's work, troubles animate/inanimate dualities. I wanted to sculpturally work with the materials said to be contained in Mary's glistening womb—glass, amber, and pearl. I'd been working with kiln-formed glass more and more, becoming interested in glass as it's materially so similar to glaze. Both are made up of silica, soda ash, and limestone. Also, interestingly, as Clare Longley pointed out, amber and pearls are both 'born of an irritant.'

Beyond this initial attraction to these shining gems, I wanted to work with this story and understand why it was told, its effects on gender and sexuality at the time, and if we are dealing with any of the residue today. Some context—in medieval European Christianity, men were perceived as being hard, crystalline, contained, and therefore superior to the 'soft, leaky' bodies of women, whose gestating bodies were seen as putrid. It was understood that wombs were like liquid wax, so they could take the impression of the man during intercourse—super sculptural! This misogynistic Christian lens needed to elevate Mary, the mother of Christ, from earthy, gross gestation, otherwise she was just another leaky woman, and how could the 'Son of God' be produced by that? It therefore became necessary to transform her fleshiness into divine mineral to reflect that 'her labour is divine work, not womb's work.'

Mary's femme fluids are transmuted into masculine rigidity. Amber and pearls were thought to be liquids suspended in solid form (much like glass is), and so offered a perfect material allegory for this transition. Goss specuates that this 'inorganic material grafted onto human flesh can be understood as sexual prosthesis.' For me, my leadlight work, *Mineral prosthesis*, is a loose sketch of this idea.

There are records that nuns at the time also shared this reading, and to the disdain of the church, were inspired to use inanimate objects in their sexual practices, often the same gem and stone materials as Mary's womb. I'm not sure if this was a solo thing or not (a subject for another day!). Clare was telling me about the medieval nun, mystic, poet, artist (polymath), and probable lesbian Hildergard of Bingen, who loved other nuns and wrote 'ecstatically' about the Virgin Mary—maybe this served as an inspiration to her, or rather was inspiration for the theory. I think it's interesting that this historic fabulation of the womb is really quite futuristic (or contemporary?), in a sense modelling a womb of queer prosthesis for people who can't gestate in a biological, textbook way. These materials were thought to contain medical properties and were also used by midwives at the time—I love this idea of being made up of that which can aid you.

HH: Some of the sculptures in the show—such as *Mineral prosthesis, Sunne*, and *Untitled (total internal reflection)* can be read as deconstructed, if not fully eviscerated, stained-glass windows. Per the above, theological comparisons have been made between a stained-glass window through which sunlight passes and the Virgin's womb—the leadlight window sometimes being used as a metaphor for the Immaculate Conception, in which Mary conceives a child whilst keeping her virginity intact, as it were, just as light passes through a pane of glass without breaking it.

AJP: Eviscerated stained glass windows—I love this! Honestly, these works are still new to me, and whilst they are being exhibited, having a public moment, they are for me, still gestating, or in process. Collecting readings helps me understand them. I was working on *Mineral prosthesis* first as a means of telling the story of Mary's womb, and then began studying, or attending to light more broadly in the others. I am really fascinated by this description of the window/womb being penetrated by sunlight, and that being the instance of conception. As a metaphor, the idea of sunlight creating life is not that esoteric/far out. Thinking about the sun as the primary source of metabolic energy loops back to my interest in energy transference in my earlier work with the krill. The loop of the krill, consuming the plastic made of fossil fuels (petroleum) that are formed under the earth-crust, as dead organisms (such as krill) decompose over millennia but still contain energy from photosynthesis.

HH: Thinking about wombs and pregnancy and transparency calls to mind ultrasound technology for imaging unborn fetuses. And also the profound politicisation of this technology—particularly in the way ultraconservative Christian groups in the United States have exploited this kind of imagery for various anti-abortion campaigns. By contrast, I'm intrigued how your stained-glass window (in *Mineral prosthesis*) has wound up being mostly lead—precisely the material that protectively shields the body's interior from X-ray vision in the different but related medical paradigm of radiography...

AJP: It is really interesting how medical imaging can work to cut the womb-haver out of the picture of the fetus, a total cut of relation. It does seem to have roots in this figuring of Mary, where she's merely the "architecture" or "clothing" for Jesus.

That's a good point! These works have become more frame, more lead than window, through their making. It just happened over time, unconsciously, but it does remind me of this note I have on my desk about how there is more and more lead in the universe as most of the heavier, unstable atoms gradually decay to lead—definitely an aside!

HH: After some experiments in the kiln for what would eventually become *Mineral prosthesis*, you settled on a linear, winding form in which small fragments of glass and avian mesh are tethered together by long strips of lead into which tiny freshwater pearls and amber have been enfolded here and there. This, as opposed to a more traditional, flat, windowpane-like structure. The way it is now, the lead line of *Mineral prosthesis* can be looped over beams in the roof or spooled on the floor. What do you like about this serpentine, seemingly endless line?

AJP: I think I keep returning to this form, likewise with the else loop, as a means of thinking through endless mutations of material. Or rather, how nothing really ever disappears, but just shifts into other forms. If I've had a break from the studio for a while or starting a new project, I often start with creating these loops of elselselselslelslelse that feed into themselves, or eat themselves. I think alot about metabolic energy, how it's forever being transferred on a cellular level.

HH: One of the things that first attracted me to your work—your plastic tubs of krill shit, petrol, scobies, and whatnot—was the relentlessness of their dirt and grime. I'm enjoying this filth factor in the little metal bowl you're using as a kind of doorstop to lever-open the avian mesh spiral in *Sunne*. But on top of this dirty orange patina is a scattering of tiny, gorgeous golden droplets of glass, which are themselves the dripping residue of your slumped glass firing technique. Can you say anything about the operation of the tiny and the gorgeous in this show? The pearls and amber enfolded in lead, the radiant glass raindrops, and little clusters of coloured glass on avian mesh?

AJP: The fibrils, droplets softened from gravel-like glass in the kiln illuminated from within, demonstrate a phenomena in physics called 'total internal reflection.' A phenomenon that can appear in droplets of rain and also determines the angles in which diamonds are cut. I'm glad you find them gorgeous!

HH: The first question I had in mind for you was around the relationship between sculpture and language or speaking. I can't stop thinking about *H ladder*, whose form reminds me of an orthodontic plate that would sit on the roof of one's mouth. You once pointed out a connection between the "H ladder" on this sculpture, which has been formed by black wire, and the 'h' in the Irish spelling of your name.

BF: Yes, there is a h which is specifically, or sometimes surprisingly, within my name. This h was introduced to me as the sound 'haitch.' I've carried a quote around for a decade or more of Hélène Cixous's in *Three Steps on the Ladder of Writing*. She says within it, 'the H in my name is a ladder ... to the depths.' This line is all that I remember from that text, so it remains enigmatic to me. Obviously it resonated because it's like an interest that I've carried on.

HH: What is the interest, specifically?

BF: I'm thinking of speech as a kind of assemblage; as continuous formation with what surfaces, and of formation as a "H ladder" with which to access depths. Okay. I'll try to talk to the sculpture and language of this work: the two flat surfaces in the sculpture are a shape cut from a photo of foam swirling upon Merri Creek, and a serviette meant to wipe up whatever was around my mouth. Both are materials that have surfaced/spoken to me, I worked with them and made this form. I can see now how they relate to depths, e.g., the deep pulse of the creek churning foam and yeah, mouth spills food, spit, and speech, and in speech spills the unconscious. And then the 'H' made of wire is hooked, and pierces through the serviette surface to hang from it. I really love working with the multi-dimensions of material in terms of my relations and associations to them.

HH: I was wondering about the relationship between your sculptural and psychoanalytic practices, which you undertake almost in tandem with one another...

BF: While making this show I wondered this too.

HH: Often in your work, materials have very specific histories attached to them, which, when known to the viewer, unfurl new associations and meanings. For example, your spiders made from balls of petrol rolled up and spewed out by the ocean, which are sprinkled with green peridots picked from the road near your family home. For this show, you've been working with another very specific material: roots that grew within the sewerage pipes underneath this family home. What made you want to work with these sewerage roots?

BF: I heard about the roots through chatting to my dad who had discovered the sewerage system was totally infiltrated with roots from the trees surrounding their house. I was thinking of this amazing presence that had lived and thrived beneath the home that I had also grown up in. We planted the trees around that house when I was four years old, so the lifespan is pretty similar to my own.

HH: Do you remember what kind of trees they were?

BF: We planted them through the process of direct seeding, scattering seeds collected locally. This included she-oaks, wattle, tea tree, eucalypts — I'm not really sure which ones made it into the pipes. Thinking of the sewerage roots as a material, I work a lot with wire and think of wire as writing — a line. The visual languages of these wiry roots really appealed to me when I finally saw them. It's kind of disgusting, but also feels very sentimental and gothic to be using family roots... But now the roots are not alive; they've been uprooted and they're brittle. They are on their way to turning into dirt.

HH: Yeah, you can tell. Do you want to say a little bit about the process of how your dad alerted you to the roots and then you asked him to keep them for you?

BF: Because of the pandemic — the restriction of the border around the city — I couldn't collect them myself. So, I asked him to keep the roots for me. When he originally pulled them out they were really long, body length. It was an amazing object. He then made what I've been calling a hammock — of metal poles and chicken wire hanging between the poles. And the roots were arrested... they looked like a body lying on a hammock through all of winter, through all of the seasons — almost a year, I think. They were thoroughly washed in the rain, and then became really brittle under the sun. And so then they were broken into bags, by the time I got them.

HH: That's right. I was going to ask you specifically about the small sculpture *eyelid*, because you had mentioned that its form relates to the hammock shape (if not the scale).

BF: Since we began planning the show, the hammock was definitely a form that I kept in mind for a long time. It dropped off at some point, but then it sort of returned with the roots in the eyelid sculpture being that same curved shape. This sculpture is called *eyelid*, but to me it is almost a membrane between consciousness and the unconscious, or also like to sleep. It's to look through an eyelid at that point where you are drifting. And I think in that way hammocks do something similar — they conjure that moment between states.

HH: Would you like to say anything about the other elements that are in *eyelid*? Like the purple shimmering eyeshadow? Or the solder? How do those other kinds of details function for you?

BF: While I speak of the *Eyelid* as internal, I was decorating it in the studio as if to make it shimmer. The solder is a very easy material to drip into a makeshift diamante, but in electronics it does connect wire. And the *Eyelid* is made up of these wire roots. That peridot is also sprinkled in there too. It may have been the act of adding violet eye shadow that created an eyelid for me. I'm not sure what comes first... but, do you know when you put your hands over your eyelids and you sort of like see colour?

HH: Totally. Funnily, I hadn't thought about sleep as having a big role to play in this body of work, but reading Autumn's poem this morning and sensing her strong emphasis on the bedside table, and then hearing you speak just now about the hammock and the closed eyelid, all of a sudden it feels central...

BF: Autumn began writing this poem in my studio one night while I was making the *Bedside table* sculpture. We were talking about the bedside table being one of those objects that kind of bears witness, but then also holds objects that you want with you between states of wake and sleep, conscious and unconscious — like a glass of water, a book, a lamp, something sexy, something medicinal... What else? The other thing to say about the sculpture *Bedside table* is that it has the most flimsy structure. It's a joke and a joy to me that it can stand.

HH: That takes me to the next point I was thinking upon. You were talking about your ongoing interest in wire and its relationship to writing, and then to wiry tree roots. In this exhibition, in several of the sculptures, you have strung up glass beads using the finest strands of your own hair... I guess hair obviously has a root?

BF: Underground, yeah. It seems like hair has this other life before it appears.

HH: Actually, in mentioning hair you just reminded me of something I didn't fully understand the resonance of in Autumn's poem...

BF: Autumn's radiant poem connects the several sculptures made from my cut hair with how the cut hair creates the haircut, in that the cut — the loss — is also where creation forms. The sculpture *Bird 1/3* includes 3 long strands of hair that aren't cut, however. They were pulled out and are almost like the length of this show, which was on/off three years in the making due to rolling lockdowns. During this time, until a summer chop, I was growing my hair.

HH: I suppose there's two different associations with hair: hair cut or shorn, or hair from the root. A bit like how you have your bag of sewerage roots, you've also got this bag of your own hair from when you recently got your haircut.

BF: Yeah, these bags of seemingly dead ends have been really generative for this body of work.

HH: Did we cover everything you wanted to say about hair as a material? It being a form of writing, and as being like the length of the show? And the fineness of it, I suppose, like, I couldn't imagine a finer material... It's so light it's almost not present.

BF: When I see a hair stuck on the shower glass with water, I often think of that as my signature.

HH: The other material that we haven't discussed yet is, of course, the plastic tree protectors or tree guards — the plastic pocket with the three wooden stakes that together protect a young sapling.

BF: I love the subtle green glow of the plastic tube and the hollow triangular prism. This show doesn't have that shape in it, the closest moment would be the centre of *Bedside table*, but I hope that this material reminds you of that shape. The sapling is also not present, and in this absence the notion of the safeguarded centre broadens or becomes a question. Sometimes in these works I've pierced through or cut the plastic protector. At the same time, I imagine all the tubes in the show could connect together to form a single long tube and loop into a torus.

HH: Oh, interesting! I recall you were keeping that one really cylindrical clump of sewerage roots inside two plastic pockets joined together on your studio floor, and it's even been at Mejia under the table during install. This is a sight that I really like; I'm so glad Beth photographed it too.

There is also the number three, which is really embedded in the structure of the tree protector, the three stakes. And it's elsewhere in the show: in one of the titles and obviously it's in the three interlinking hula hoops of *Bedside table*.

BF: Three, I recognise that number/form in several past works of mine as well. Here, I've made an obvious reference to the Lacanian Borromean knot. Creating this structure with hula hoops held together with twisted wire and loops of the plastic tubes is my way to play and move with it. I find Lacan's non-hierarchical linking of real, symbolic, and imaginary with the subject to be more destabilising and generative, the more I learn.

HH: The form of the knot here is important. And because I don't know anything about Borromean knots, or Lacan for that matter, I ended up reading an article on knots in philosophy and mathematics. And the part that I got the most out of was this point that there are two ways to understand the ontology of a knot: on the one hand, a knot is this thing that can join two separate entities together through the act of knotting or tying; but knots can also, in mathematical terms, designate their own boundedness or set themselves apart from the world. I guess you can read both into the Borromean knot structure...

BF: Everything being profoundly intertwined, and also totally its own. I try to relate to each material's specificities including, of course, my own. I think whenever I lean into metaphor in the work, it visualises my struggle with this. But at the same time too, um, what do you make of intertwined uniqueness?

HH: Okay. The last question I had in mind was about the colour orange — that being in the paint pigment on the sunset work (*Untitled*, 2022), in the hula hoops, and in the frottage drawing as part of *Bedside table*. But also the colour orange also links to some of your past works: the dipped spider feet, like the one on my desk at home, and the works you made at West Space from orange peels.

BF: Yeah, I made a swing from a piece of orange peel I had eaten while installing, which was anchored down by two bags of oranges. It also had these, like, dried-peel flowers sewn to the bag's mesh. The colour in that show appeared with the fruit. I think you mentioned that Derek Jarman quote about the colour orange earlier...

HH: 'What came first? The colour or the name or the fruit?'

BF: It's a fruitful question! How it shows a yearning to place the essence of an encounter in time. If I ask it, orange dissolves the answer.

HH: It also makes me think of — mind you, I don't know if this is even true — that in English, you can't rhyme any words with 'orange,' it's just sort of this annoying category of word that frustrates poets.

BF: Haha, I love it. Let's end here.

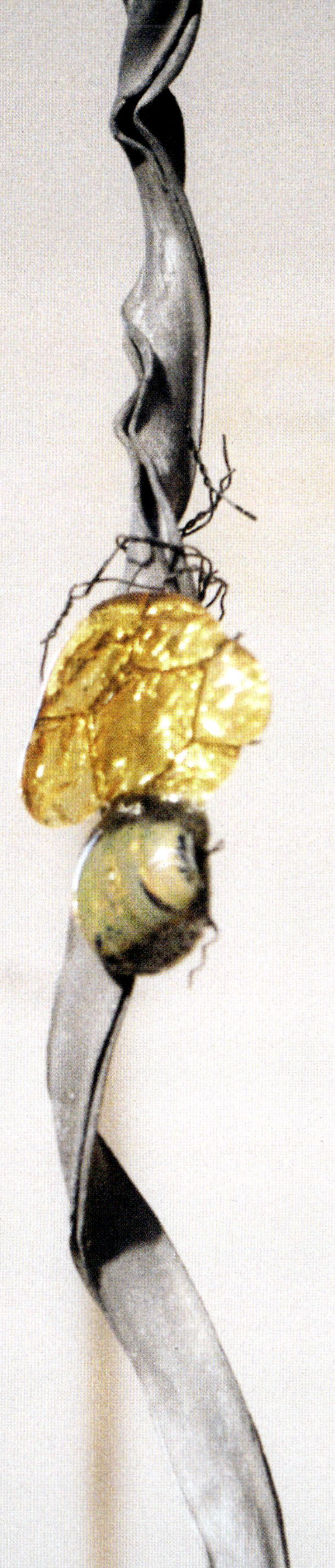

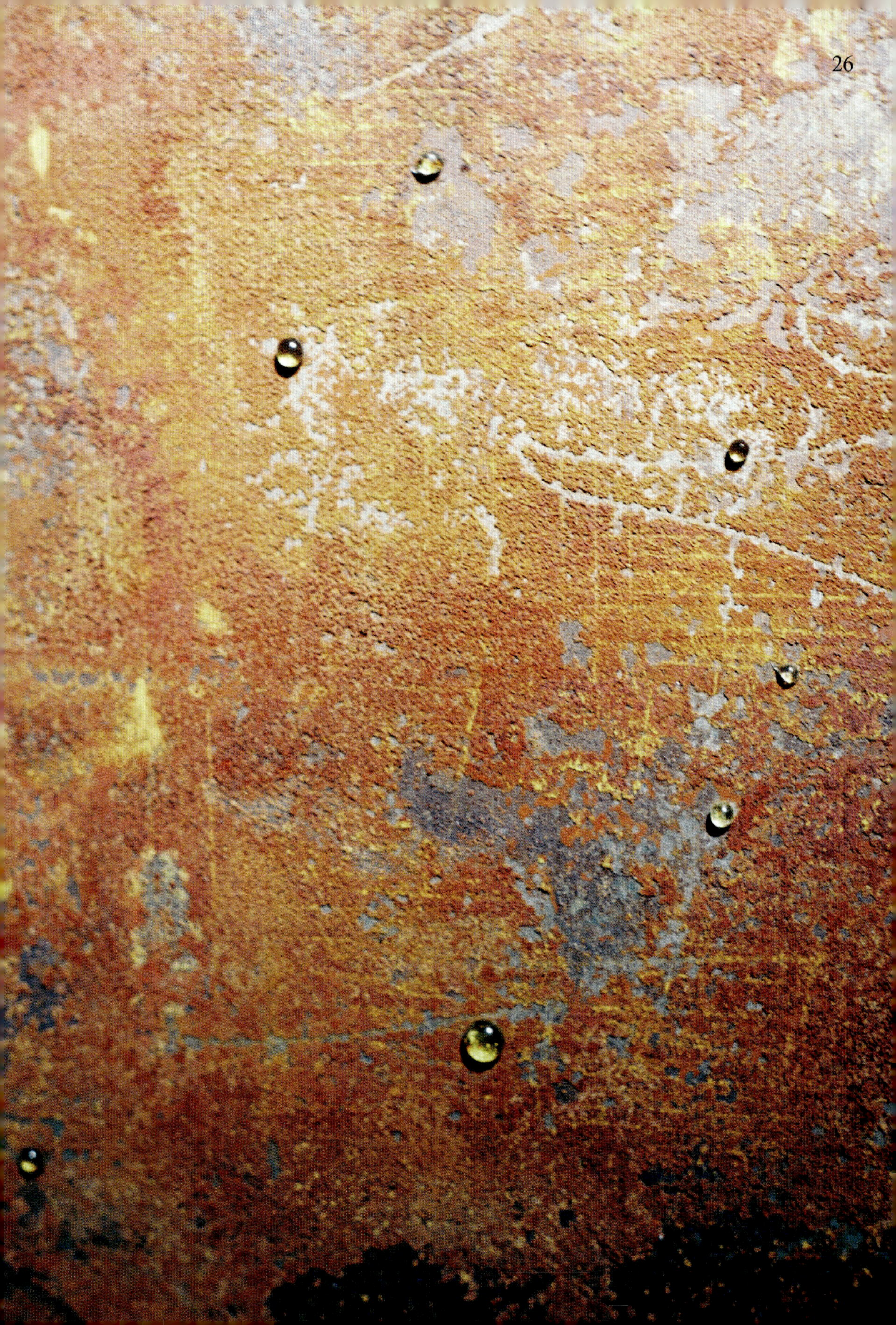

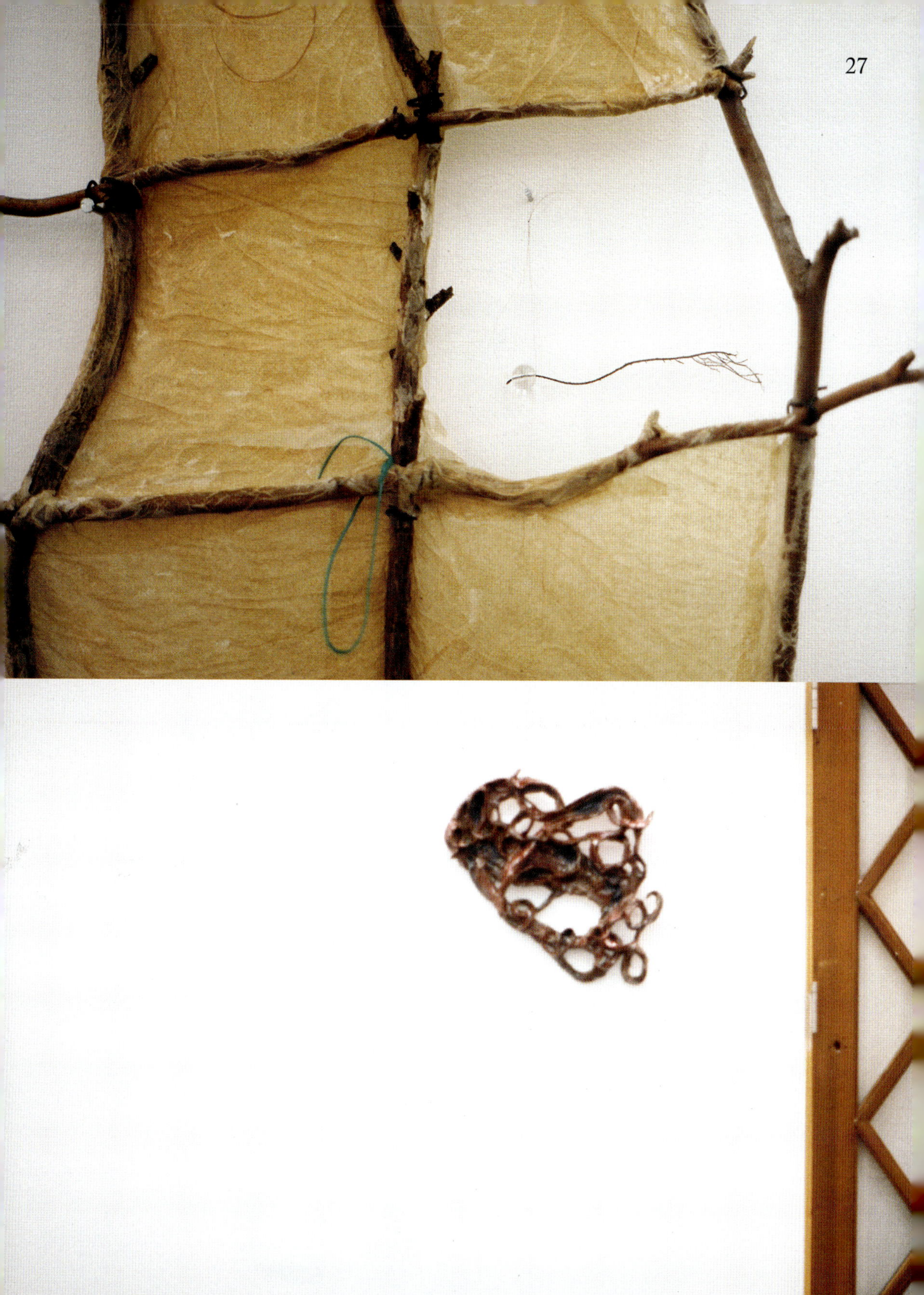

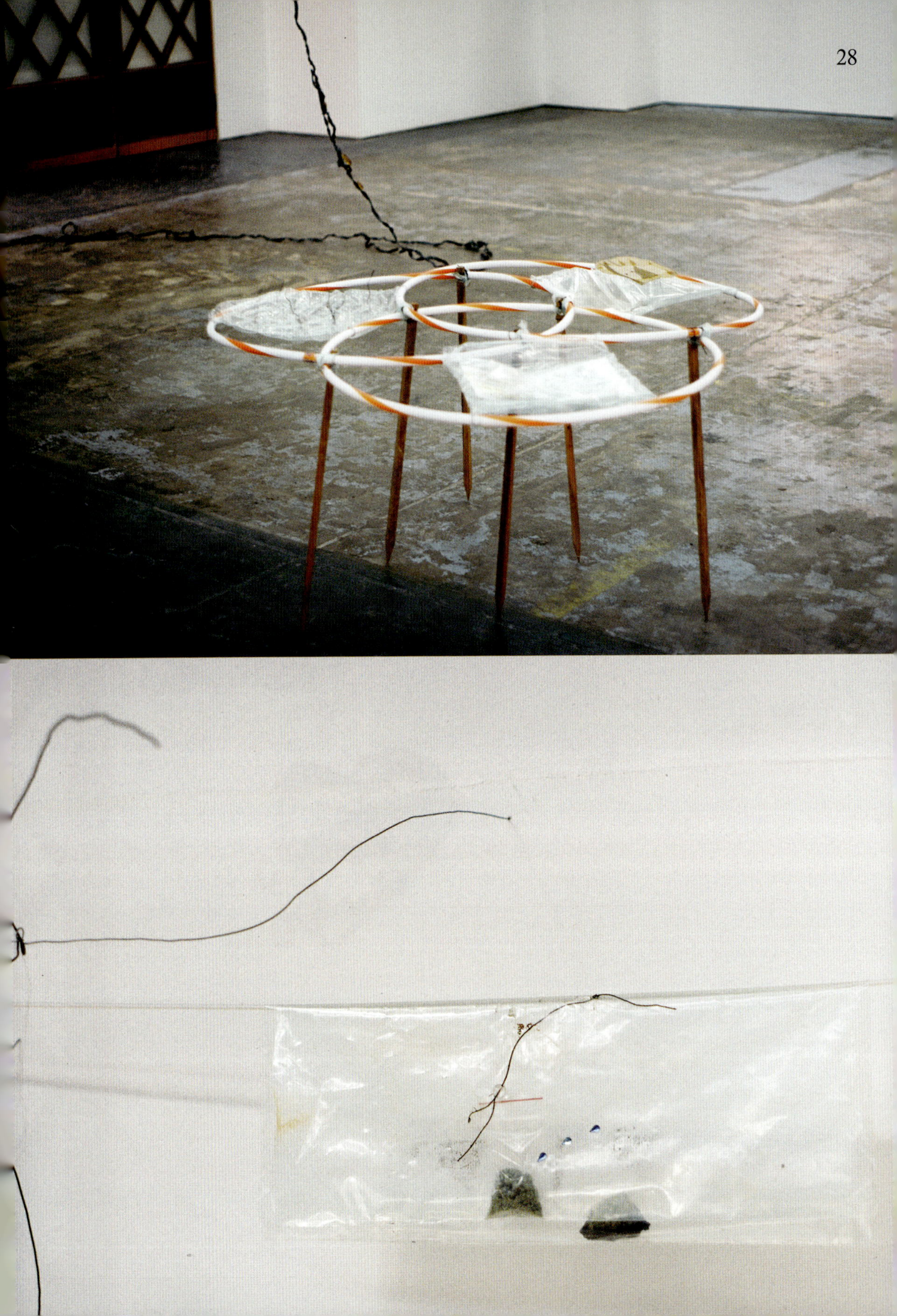

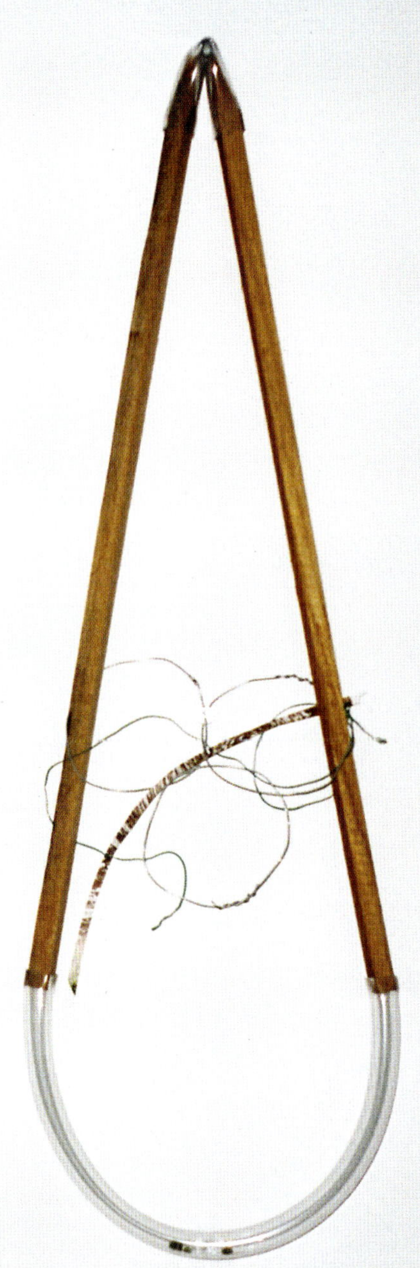

1.
The magical girl has learned how to transport light from one place to another.
Her skill is in collecting it without damaging any of its strength or capabilities.
She places these cells of light into her bag, to place on the table at home.
She arranges them in a calculated sequence, which allows them to take dimension and become a solid form.
Light is like a biography of survival, in that whatever object it passes through, its effects remain lawful and true.
She uses the method of rearranging light to help her understand time as nonlinear.
She calls her doctor who tells her, *sometimes we do not recognise change for what it is. It happens and we merely observe the Earth moving, plates shifting, it's tectonic.*

2.
My father lives in another world called Paradise. It is a place where he cooks, thinks about his grandmother, and travels through time.
One day, he tells me, *Heaven is not a place you go to but a status that you can achieve here and now.*
I understand what he is trying to tell me but I don't quite know how to achieve it.
We live in two separate worlds, which means our structures are very different.
We may both contain genetic sequences, but mine hold many more of his memories than his do of mine.
He tells me that only after I achieve the status of Heaven will he gift me another memory.
I ask him, *why not before?*
He says, *I'm afraid if I give it to you beforehand, you will deliver it to the angels.*

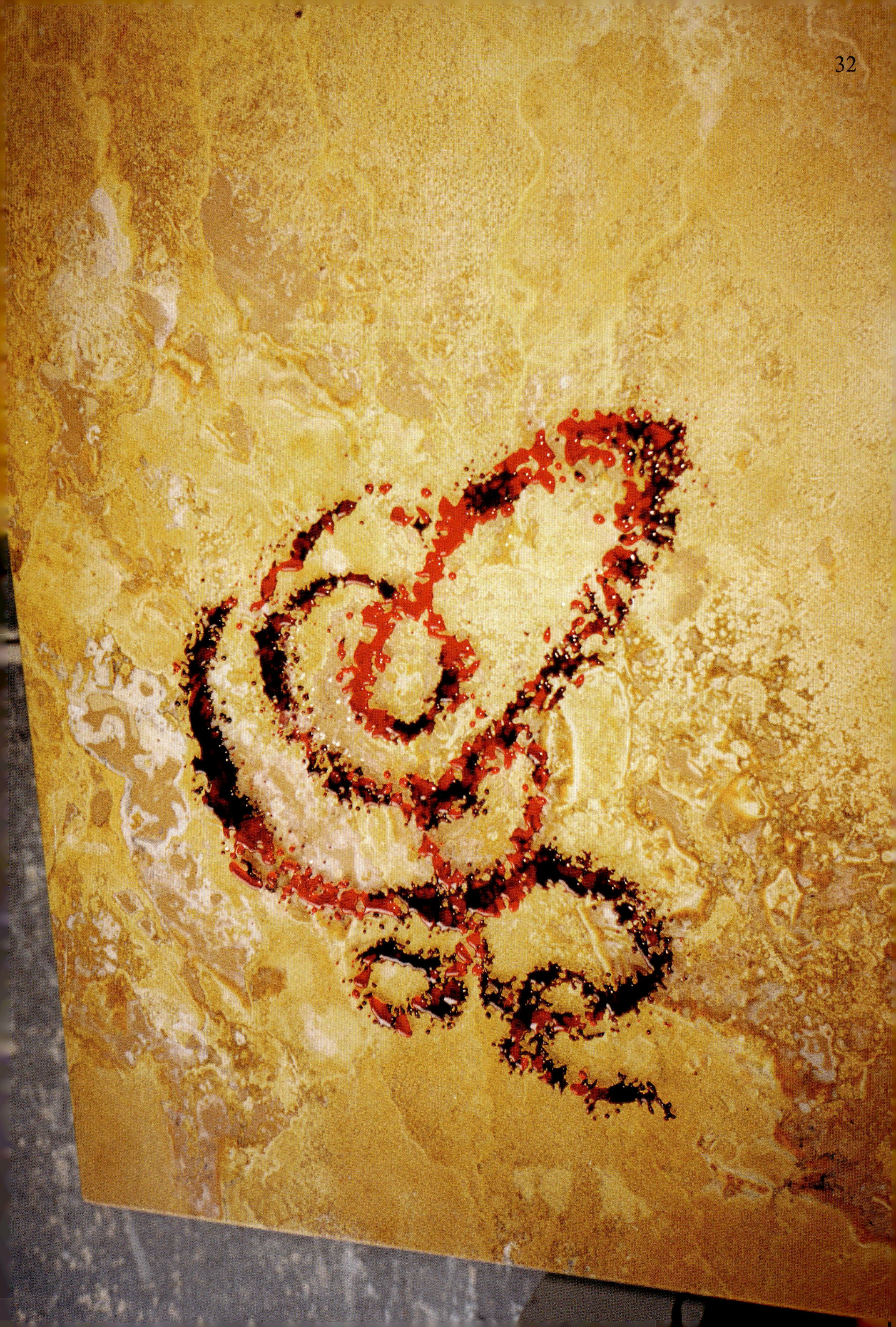

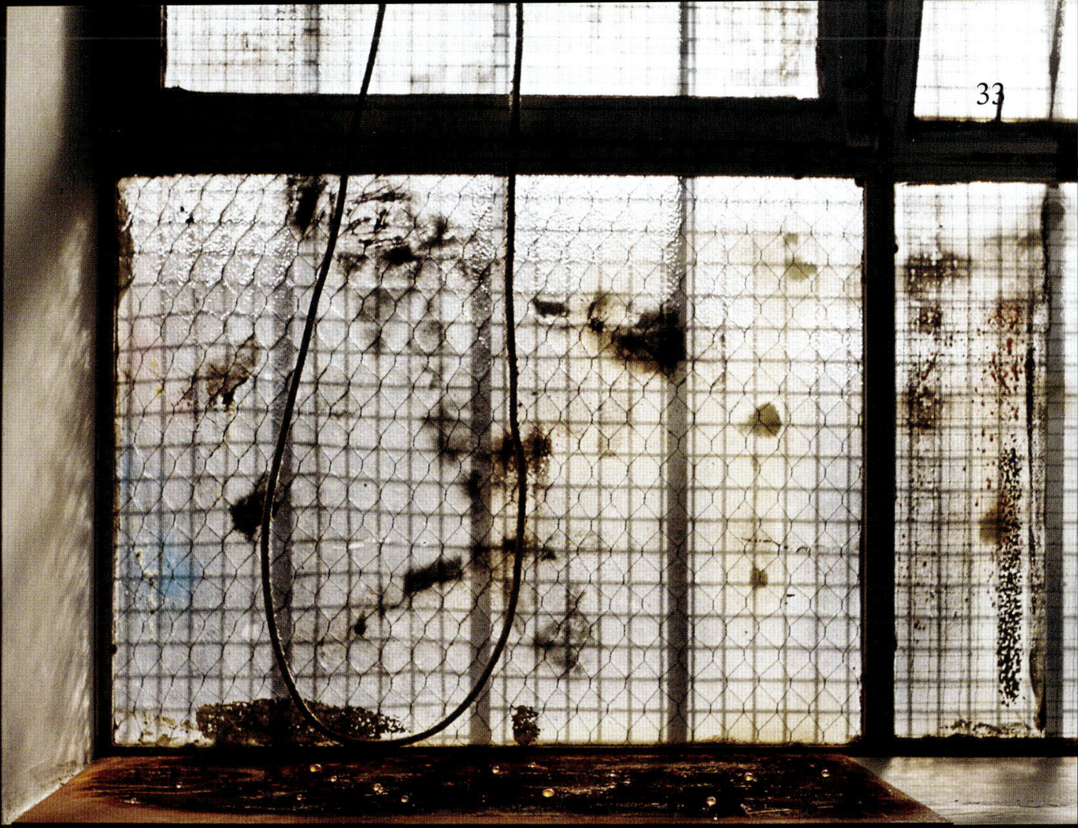

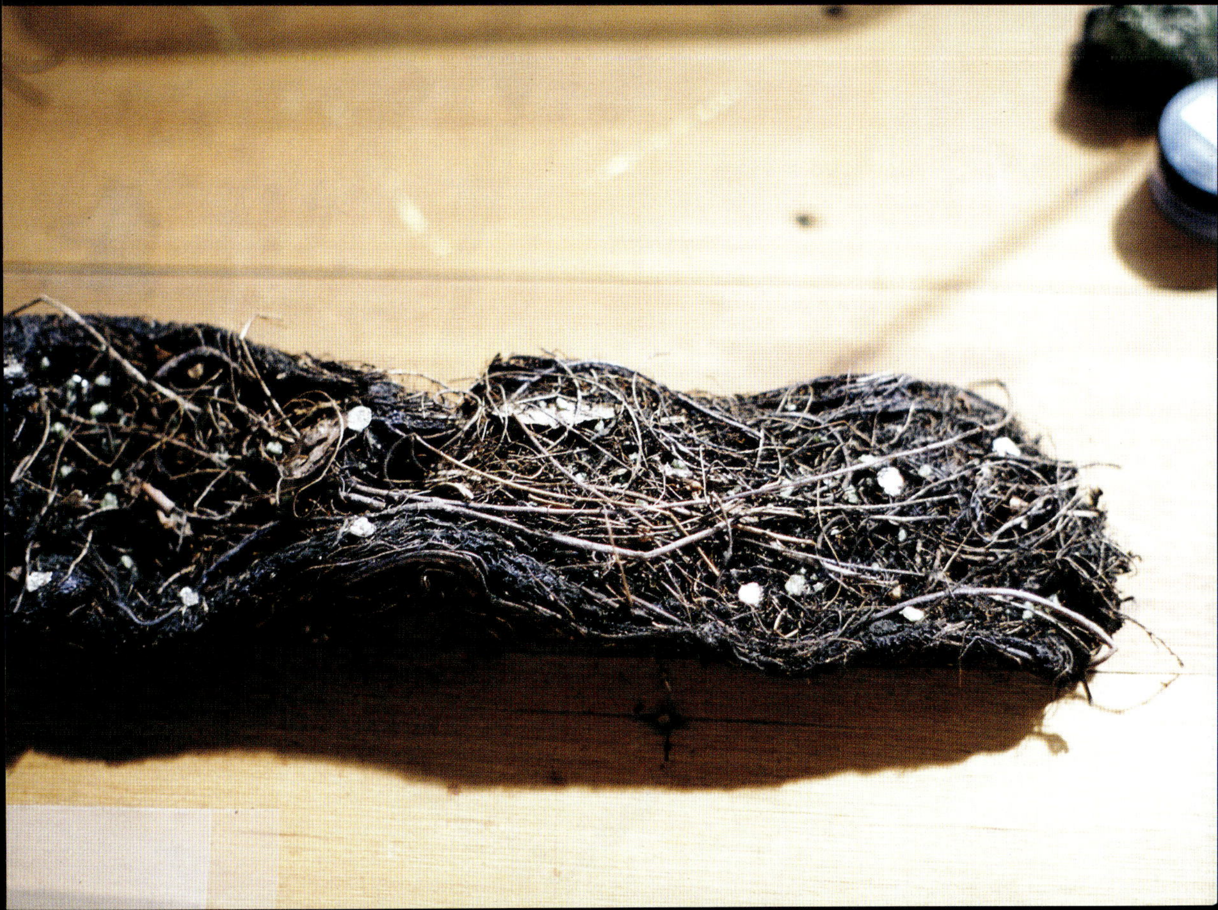

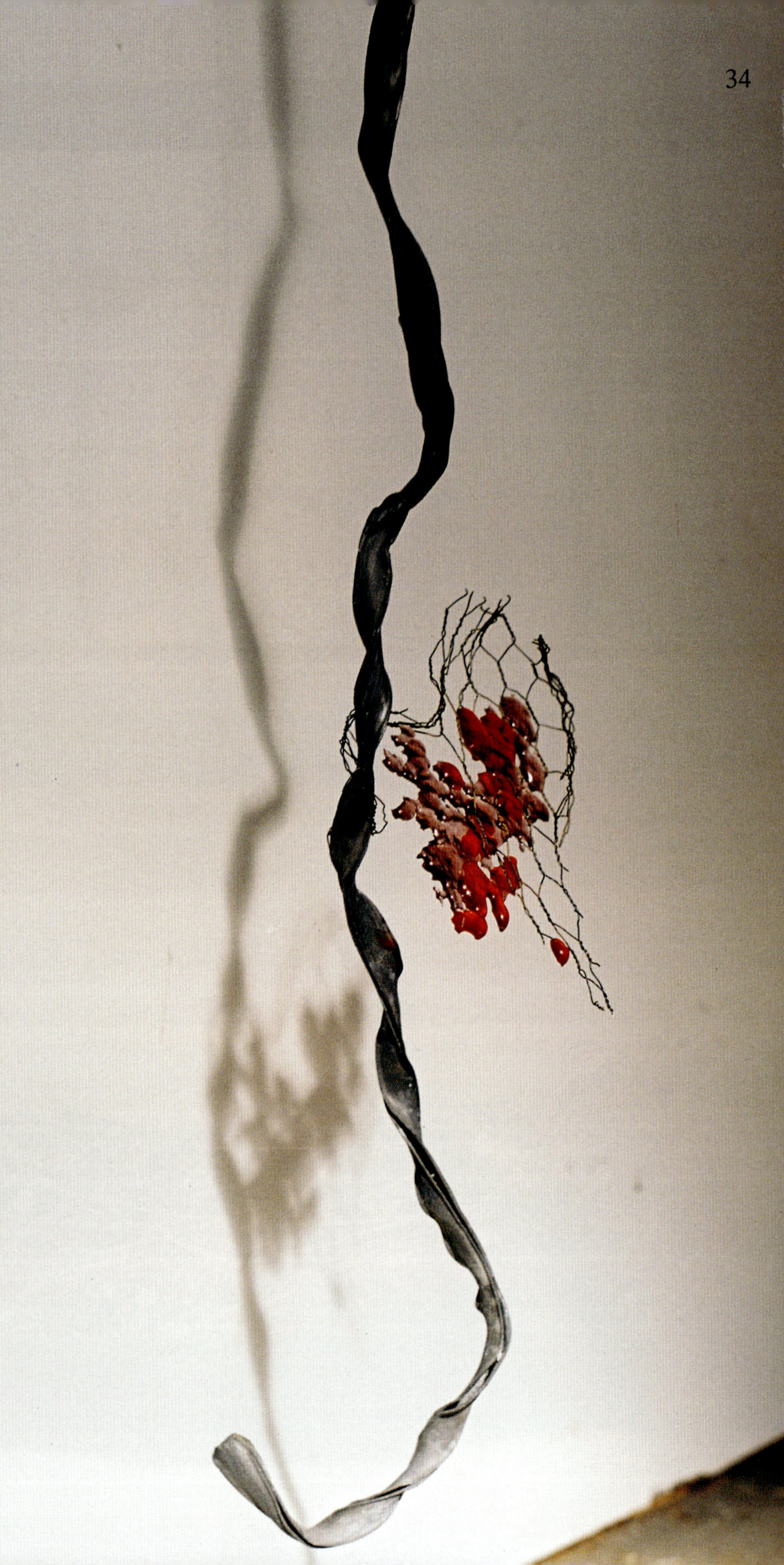

The space is austere and square, a four-sided nowhere. There are disproportionately large precious stones in the square, they are the only things there except the men, just men and nothing. One giant pearl, one giant amber-coloured stone, and another giant crystal, each covered in a thin film of something that could be blood, but no one is really sure. Mary is there, but she disappears quite often, she is not there like the other things.

The precious stones are unusual not only for their size but also for their nature and function. They are physically imperceptible but large in the mind. They are there insofar as they block all entry or possible escape. This does not stop the men trying to leave quite often, for it is quite easy to forget that they exist, particularly when they know there is another side, for that must be where Mary, or someone else yet to be identified, gets the painkillers and the bread and everything else that they find in the square, from time to time.

However leaving is impossible, instead they just writhe. When there are lots of men writhing or twitching in the square we know this is because they are trying to escape, or that they are thinking about it. The scene often occurs in slow motion, as though they were being controlled by something other than themselves. It would be logical to think that Mary controlled them, because after all, most men think that the stones belong to her, but none of them can be sure that Mary is anything other than their own invention. If she did indeed exist, she would be watching them with a compassion no less minimal than her hypothetical painkillers and bread.

The men think that the stones belong to Mary because they imagine that they were once a part of her, and that one day she left them there, and for that reason it's only her that can pass through them, as though they were bits of her flesh somehow disassociated from her body. When the men started to think in this way, it wasn't much for them to then assume that they were either Mary's food, or Mary's children, and that their existence amounted to being eaten or born. That the square was either a womb or a mouth. Passing through the stones would either mean glory or condemnation, either way a justification for their suffering.

This kind of thinking went along with other actions that occupied their days, like cleaning the blood-like substance off the stones, polishing them, looking at their own reflection. For the men, waiting for their sacrifice was their sacrifice, writhing and never thinking that maybe the stones could pass through them, that maybe they too all had a womb or a mouth as big as Mary's.

My mother's mother died in her sleep, a single mother of six. They placed her into the Earth last week, but I was not there so I could only think about her and how skies do leak.
Chi Tran

I look up and across, to gain a sense of feeling that I am
moving along. Looking out releases
my boundaries, and I continue working toward a mission of
wholeness. Some people don't believe in the conscious
order of feeling—which is to say, feeling occurs
chronologically and with entelechial intentions.
I understand why others don't, but I think I do believe in it.
I strive to work from feeling, from sensing vibrations, heat,
and the energies of light. I focus in on what could become
information and ask it to be my kin.
I try not to feel embarrassed to move or be clumsy, leak,
sweat or bleed. I may be surveilled while leaking from the
body but it does not stop me from collecting my own
deposits. If the matter in my line of vision is held long
enough in the light,
I can shift my perspective and it will restructure the
molecules.
My mother's mother died in her sleep, a single mother of
six. They placed her into the Earth last week, but I was
not there so I could only think about her and how skies
do leak.
My prayers now feel multiplied, directions of care
diversified, and my spirit expanded. It begins to rain and
I realise that the sky is not as solid as it can appear, or as I
hope for it to be.

side by side by side:
Brighid Fitzgerald | Amy Parker
Edited by Helen Hughes

1–23 April 2022

MEJIA
33 Tinning Street
Brunswick VIC 3055
mejia.com.au

ISBN 978-0-9945388-3-3

Edition of 200.
Printed by Printgraphics, Naarm/Melbourne.

Published by Discipline, Naarm/Melbourne.
discipline.net.au

Designed by James Oates.

Texts by Brighid Fitzgerald, Helen Hughes, Aodhan Madden, Beth Maslen, James Oates, Amy Jane Parker, Autumn Royal, and Chi Tran.

Photography by Beth Maslen.

Acknowledgements

Discipline operates on the sovereign, unceded land of the Wurundjeri people of the Kulin Nation. We honour Wurundjeri Ancestors and Elders, past, present, and emerging. Always was, always will be Aboriginal land.

Warmest thanks to Claudia and Nicolas Mejia for the opportunity to develop and present the exhibition that this book accompanies. Thanks kindly to Sarah Ujmaia for the paper-mulcher, Marian Crawford for paper advice, and Joel Stern for interview transcription.

Contributors

Brighid Fitzgerald is an artist living in Naarm/Melbourne.

Helen Hughes is a Senior Lecturer in the Fine Art department at Monash University where she coordinates Honours in Art History, Theory, and Curatorial Practice.

Aodhan Madden is an artist and a writer.

Beth Maslen is an artist from Perth currently living and working in Naarm/Melbourne.

James Oates is a designer based in Naarm/Melbourne.

Amy Jane Parker is an artist and an access and inclusion worker at Footscray Community Arts Centre in Naarm/Melbourne.

Autumn Royal creates drama, poetry, and criticism.

Chi Tran is a writer, editor, artist and filmmaker who is interested in researching language as an active lifeform. Chi's work is highly influenced by physics, faith, genetic memory and film.

Credits

On learning a form of devotion 11 2018, by Chi Tran

This work was originally published by Recess in 2018, alongside Brighid Fitzgerald's video *linger*.

A prayer to cleanse the heart (variation ii) 2021, by Chi Tran

This work was originally commissioned in July, 2021 by Rudi Williams for her exhibition *unfixed* at Sutton Gallery.

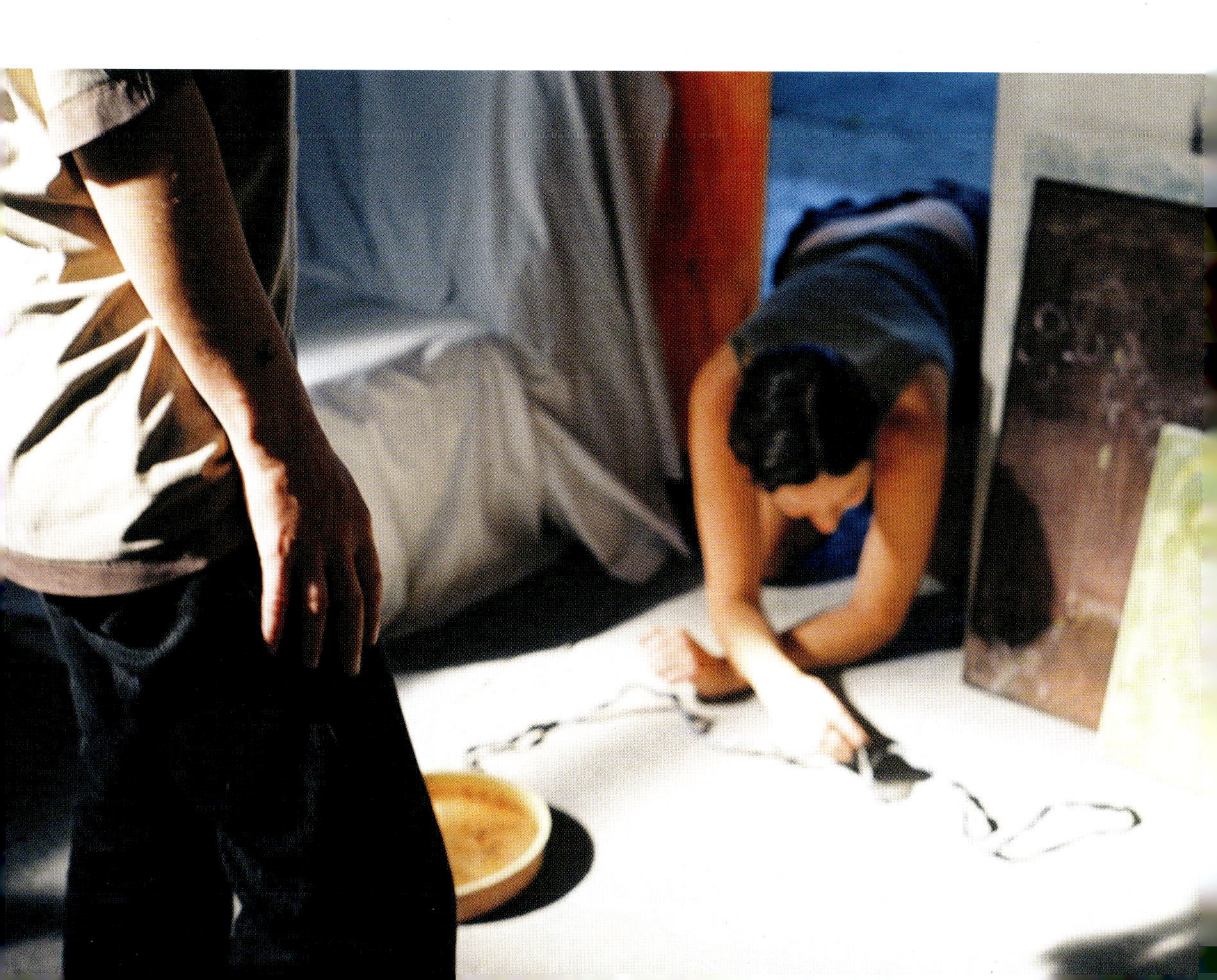

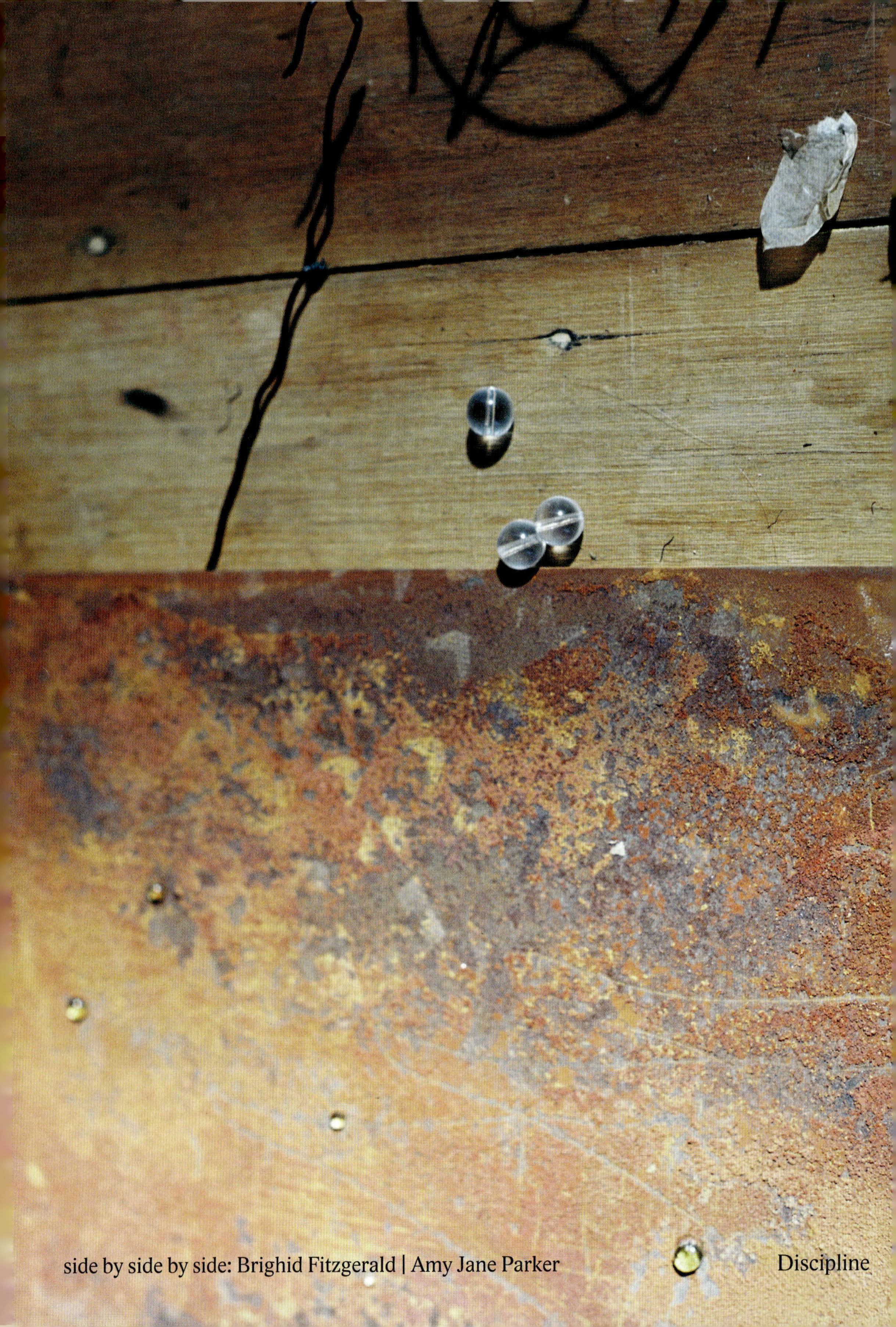

side by side by side
Brighid Fitzgerald | Amy Jane Parker
Edited by Helen Hughes

Text

7. Introduction
Helen Hughes

11. On learning a form of devotion
Chi Tran

13. Approaching a bedside table I, II, III
Autumn Royal

17. There Is No Such Thing as Elsewhere:
Amy Jane Parker Interviewed by Helen Hughes

21. A Fruitful Question:
Brighid Fitzgerald Interviewed by Helen Hughes

31. A Prayer to cleanse the heart (variation ii)
Chi Tran

35. NANOPARTICLES
Aodhan Madden

37. My mother's mother died in her sleep, a single mother of six. They placed her into the Earth last week, but I was not there so I could only think about her and how skies do leak.
Chi Tran

Image

All photography by Beth Maslen.

4. Amy Jane Parker, *Untitled (total internal reflection)*, 2022
Steel, glass

4, 16, 28, 33. Installation view, MEJIA

1, 5, 9, 12, 16, 26, 28, 33, 34, 39, 40.
Studio documentation, 27.03.21

5. Brighid Fitzgerald, *Untitled*, 2022
Hose, crude oil, octopus clip, peridot, glass beads, water

12. Brighid Fitzgerald, *Bedside table*, 2022; featuring *H sculpture*, 2022
Wooden stakes, plastic tree guard, sewerage roots, wire, glass beads, hula hoops, paper, pencil; wire, paper, serviette, PVA glue

26, 33. Amy Jane Parker, *Mineral prosthesis*, 2022
Lead, glass, amber, steel, pearls

18, 25. Amy Jane Parker, *Sunne*, 2022
Glass, steel, rust

27. Brighid Fitzgerald, *Ladder*, 2022
Sticks, serviettes, wire, gardening twine, hair, plastic tree guard, PVA glue, glass bead

27. Amy Jane Parker, *elselslelslelselselse*, 2022
Copper, glazed stoneware, oil

29. Brighid Fitzgerald, *Drop*, 2022
Hose, wooden stakes, glass beads, wire, garden twine, paper, peridot

32. Amy Jane Parker, *else loop*, 2022
Glass

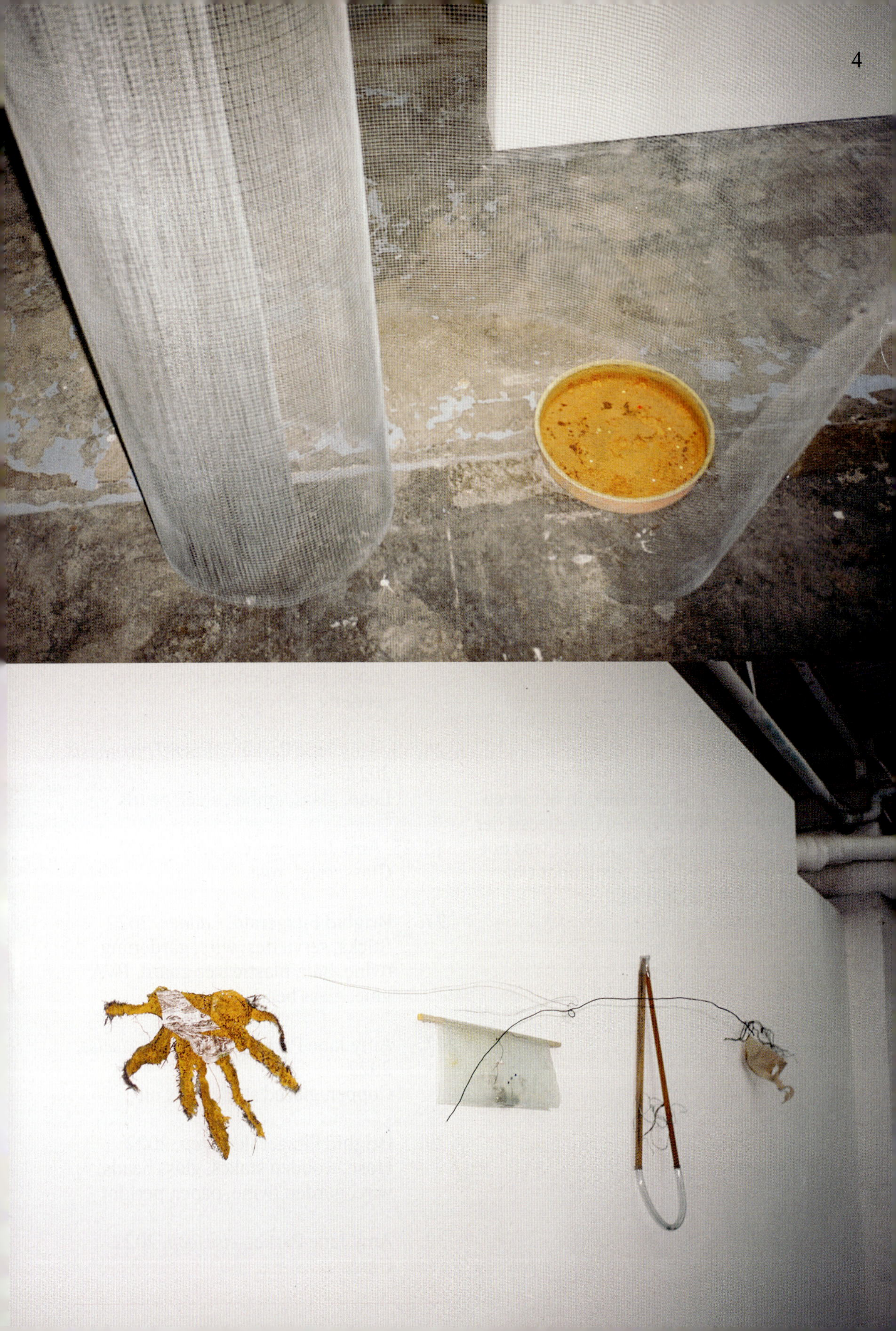

4

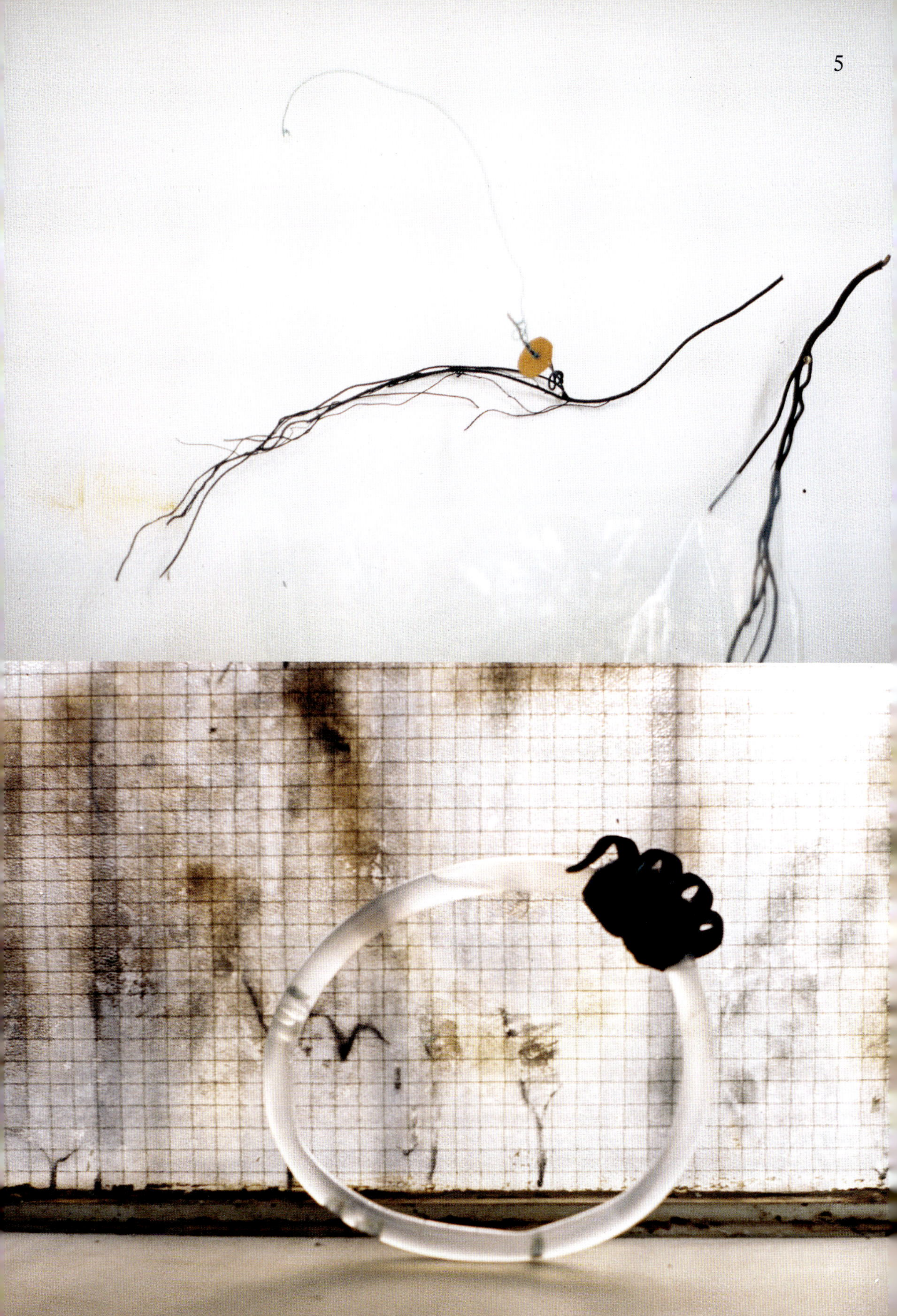